■SCHOLASTIC

Tunes That Teach
American History

10 Lively Tunes and Hands-On Activities
That Teach About Important Events in
American History

by Ken Sheldon

NEW YORK • TORONTO • LONDON • AUCKLAND • SYDNEY

MEXICO CITY • NEW DELHI • HONG KONG • BUENOS AIRES

Teaching *Resources*

Credits

As always, many thanks to Sean Flemming for his technical and personal support. Thanks also to Dana Shellmire and Dave Nelson (vocalists), the Tea Party Chorale (Dave Nelson, Tim Lowry, and Tom Bielecki), and the Forest Road Choir: Tom, Emily, and Matt Bates; Beth and Anne Marie Beaudin; Jim, Ellen, and Emily Bingham; Kathy and Matty Birkebaak; Kathy, Bill, and Molly Channon; Sarah, Alice, and Owen Hale; Lisa, Peter, Genna, and Jordan Hoekstra; Skip, Libby, and Christy Iltis; Rose and Tim Lowry; Dave, Margaret, Emily, Averill, and Nora Nelson; Elizabeth Nicholson; and Chris Sheldon (the Sweetie Supreme). This project was mastered at Blue Planet Studio, Swanzey, NH.

Helen Rosenthal's impressions of coming to America on "Where Are We Going?" are courtesy of the Oral History Project at the Ellis Island Immigration Museum.

This recording is dedicated to the memory of my grandparents: Amadeo Giovannacci came to this country from Italy at the age of four; Vinnie Davison moved here from Nova Scotia with her family; Georgie Rich came from a sailing family in Marblehead, Massachusetts; and Albert Sheldon's ancestors missed the boat (the *Mayflower*), but caught the next one, coming to America in the 1600s.

You can hear samples of all my Scholastic recordings at www.kensheldon.com.

Cover design by Maria Lilja
Cover illustration by Debbie Palen
Interior design by Jeffrey Dorman
Interior illustrations by Jenny Williams
Teacher activities written by Amy Miller

Book ISBN 0-439-38521-0
Product ISBN 0-439-38520-2

1 2 3 4 5 6 7 8 9 10   40   12 11 10 09 08 07 06 05

Table of
Contents

Introduction

History can be one of the most fascinating subjects taught in school. What can be more exciting than tales of adventurous explorers, noble natives, fearless cowboys, and brave soldiers? When teachers know how to bring history to life, engage students' imaginations, and fill students with a desire to know more about people and times, learning becomes less of a chore and more of an exploration.

Tunes That Teach American History is designed to help you engage the imaginations of your students. Using humor, drama, and a variety of musical styles, the songs in this book and CD aim to draw listeners into the fascinating times and people in our history. Each song deals with a specific event or era of American history, though the topics were chosen to fit in with broader themes in standard curricula.

While it's impossible for a song to provide all the facts about a historical event, we've tried to make the songs as accurate as possible. In addition, we've provided background information that you can share with students before or after listening to each song. You'll also find extension activities, some with companion reproducible pages, to help students delve into that time in history even more.

We've also done something new with this recording and included background "sing along" tracks (minus the main vocal) for each of the songs, so that students can enter more fully into the stories. Feel free to use these tracks for assemblies or other performances and make your students the stars.

History boring? Never again!

Ken Sheldon

Background & Activities

Welcome to the New World
(Exploration)

The first European explorers arrived in the "new world" in the late 1400s. With newfound wealth and technology, they came in search of trade routes to Asia for the growing populations of England, Spain, and Portugal. Instead, they found a new continent with vast kingdoms of indigenous peoples.

Funded by the monarchs of Spain and Portugal, Christopher Columbus set sail for Asia in 1492. He landed on a Caribbean island in the Bahamas, thinking he had reached the East Indies. Italian Amerigo Vespucci reached the northern coast of South America in 1499 and pronounced the land a new continent, which European mapmakers named "America" in his honor.

In 1523, Spanish explorer Vasco Núñez de Balboa became the first European to see the Pacific Ocean. That same year, Juan Ponce de León, another Spaniard, explored the Bahamas and Florida, searching for a fountain of youth. In 1543, Jacques Cartier explored almost the entire Atlantic Coast of the present United States for France. English sea captain Henry Hudson traveled up the Hudson River in 1609, and explored Hudson Strait and Hudson Bay the following year. French-Canadian explorer Louis Jolliet led an expedition down the Mississippi River in 1673.

While many explorers continued to look for a fast route to Asia, others began thinking of conquering the gold- and silver-rich empires of the Americas. Spaniard Hernán Cortés invaded Mexico in 1519 and defeated the Aztec. Francisco Pizarro conquered Peru's Inca Empire in 1532. But it wasn't just superior military might that destroyed the native kingdoms of the Americas. European diseases such as smallpox, measles, and influenza killed millions of Native Americans. Scholars estimate that the Native American population dropped 90 percent in the first century of contact, largely due to disease.

To Do

Assign each student an explorer to research, or invite students to choose one. Photocopy and distribute "Explorer Fact Cube" (page 15) to each student, and ask students to follow the directions on the sheet to create a fact cube about their explorer. Display students' finished work on a table or shelf.

The People of the Land
(Native Americans)

The Native Americans who greeted the first Europeans were diverse groups of people. They spoke between 300 and 350 different languages, and their cultures varied widely.

In the years that followed, disease and war killed millions of Native Americans and destroyed their cultures. In North America, the final blows came in the 1800s when thousands of white settlers arrived, seeking farmland and pushing out the native tribes.

The once mighty Iroquois of the Northeast, which included the Mohawk, Oneida, Onondaga, Cayuga, and Seneca tribes, were forced to live on reservations near Buffalo and Syracuse in New York in the early 1800s. The national government pressured the 60,000 remaining Cherokee, Choctaw, Chickasaw, Creek, and Seminole in the South to sell their land for pennies an acre and move west. In 1830, Congress passed the Indian Removal Act, which offered Native Americans living east of the Mississippi River federal land in the West. Many accepted, but many did not. The U.S. Army evicted more than 18,000 Cherokee still living in the South in 1838, and forcibly removed them 1,000 miles to a reservation in what is now Oklahoma. More than 4,000 people died in what would become known as the Trail of Tears.

After the Civil War, more white settlers headed west through the Great Plains, where the Blackfoot, Sioux, Dakota, Cheyenne, Comanche, Arapaho, Navajo, and Apache lived. The settlers not only brought diseases, they killed off vast buffalo herds on which Native Americans had depended for survival. The Plains peoples defended their land from federal troops, and fierce battles took place in the 1860s and 1870s.

Shoshone Indians also rebelled against the Mormons who were moving into their land in Utah. In January 1865 a U.S. Army force defeated the Shoshone in the Battle of Bear River, killing about 250 Shoshones, including 90 women and children.

Chief Joseph, leader of the Nez Percé in Wallowa Valley, Oregon, led nearly 800 Nez Percé on an escape route to Canada as 2,000 U.S. soldiers chased them. They traveled more than a thousand miles in the dead of winter before being captured on October 5, 1877 at Bear Paw Mountain in Montana, only 40 miles from the Canadian border.

In 1890 at the Battle of Wounded Knee, federal troops fired on a group of Sioux, massacring more than 300 men, women, and children. The battle marked the end of Native American resistance to settlement.

To Do

In the 1800s, many Native American tribes suffered the anguish and loss of being forcibly removed by the United States government from the land their ancestors had inhabited for hundreds of years. Divide the class into six groups and assign each group one of the following tribes: the Nez Percé, Cherokee, Bannocks, Cheyenne, Sioux, or Paiute. Ask students to conduct research on their tribe and find out where the tribe's original homeland was and to where they were moved. Have students trace the tribe's removal path on a map of the United States. Invite each group to report on their findings, including these questions: How many miles did the tribe travel? How many died along the way?

The Tea and the Taxes
(American Revolution)

Great Britain established its colonies in North America by the 1700s, but did little to govern them. Its government wanted only to profit from the trade of commodities such as sugar and tobacco.

The British government did believe that Parliament had the power to tax the colonies to help pay for wars in America and in Europe. But colonists had created their own local governments and thought only their elected representatives should have the power to levy taxes.

Tensions erupted in the 1760s when Parliament passed a series of taxes to help pay for the French and Indian War. In 1764, Parliament passed the Sugar Act and in 1765, the Stamp Act, which required all legal documents, licenses, commercial contracts, newspapers, pamphlets, dice, and playing cards to have a tax stamp. Colonists protested the Stamp Act so much that Parliament repealed it one year later.

In 1767, Parliament passed the Townshend Acts, which imposed duties on tea, lead, paper, glass, and paint. They also strengthened the British government's power to collect taxes. Americans rioted in the streets and boycotted all British goods, particularly tea. The British responded by sending troops to Boston, the center of colonial resistance, for the next year and a half. On March 5, 1770, British soldiers fired into a mob of Americans, killing five men. On the day of the Boston Massacre, Parliament repealed all the Townshend Acts, except the one on tea.

Colonists began smuggling tea from Holland. When the British government made it possible to sell its tea cheaper than Holland's, colonists disguised as Native Americans dumped 342 chests of tea into Boston Harbor on December 16, 1773. This event became known as the Boston Tea Party.

With the Intolerable Acts of 1774, Britain closed Boston Harbor until Bostonians paid for the tea. The acts also permitted British soldiers to stay in civilian households and abolished the elected legislature in Massachusetts. It had become clear that Britain would use military force to subdue its colonies.

To Do

Invite students to make a flip chart that tells about some of the major events and people of the American Revolution. Photocopy and distribute the "American Revolution Flip Chart" (page 16) and a blank sheet of copy paper to each student. Have students follow the directions to create their own flip charts.

Answers:
1. George Washington 2. The Stamp Act 3. Boston 4. King George III
5. Crispus Attucks 6. 342 7. Samuel Adams

The Bill of Rights Rag
(Bill of Rights)

In May 1786, after the United States won its independence from Great Britain, 55 delegates representing every state but Rhode Island convened in Philadelphia and drew up a Constitution of the United States. The Constitution balanced power between large and small states, and among three branches of government: legislative, executive, and judicial. The authors created a two-house legislature, or Congress, a president, and a Supreme Court to govern the new republic. They also carefully separated the powers of the three branches and established checks and balances between them.

The proceedings of the Constitutional Convention were kept secret until September 1787. Then it was sent to state conventions elected for the purpose of *ratifying*, or approving, the Constitution. A battle quickly ensued between Federalists, who supported the Constitution and a strong central government, and anti-Federalists, who feared a strong national government. They were particularly distrustful of a Constitution that lacked a bill of rights protecting the rights of citizens.

By 1788 all states, with the exception of North Carolina and Delaware, had ratified the Constitution, with the promise that the new government would enact a bill of rights. Congress ultimately passed 12 amendments to the Constitution. Ten were ratified and became known as the Bill of Rights.

The First Amendment protects the freedoms of speech, press, assembly, and religion from federal legislation. The second guarantees the right to bear arms, and the third makes it difficult for the government to house soldiers in citizens' homes. The fourth through eighth amendments define a citizen's rights in court and under arrest. The ninth states that these rights do not endanger other rights, and the tenth amendment says that any powers not granted to the national government will remain with the states and citizens.

To Do

Flash cards can help students remember what right each amendment in the Bill of Rights protects. Pair up students and give each pair 10 index cards. On one side of the cards, have students label the cards First Amendment, Second Amendment, and so on until the Tenth Amendment. Ask students to research and write the rights each amendment protects on the flip side of the corresponding card. When students are finished, ask them to quiz each other.

Grand Adventure
(Lewis and Clark)

In 1803, France sold President Thomas Jefferson a huge expanse of land that stretched from the Mississippi River to the Pacific Ocean. It was known as the Louisiana Purchase. Soon after, Jefferson began planning an expedition.

In May 14, 1804, U.S. Army officers Meriwether Lewis and William Clark left St. Louis, Missouri, and traveled about 8,000 miles to the Pacific Ocean. Both had wilderness experience and had served in Army campaigns against Native Americans. Clark had considerable mapmaking skills, and Lewis had studied plants and animals. With about 50 men and several canoes, they journeyed up the Missouri River, across the Rocky Mountain, and along the Columbia River to the Pacific Coast.

Their guide was a 19-year-old Shoshone woman named Sacagawea. She helped the expedition identify landmarks and negotiate with Native American tribes, who were suspicious of the white explorers. But not all their encounters were hostile. In mid-August of 1805, they met a band of Shoshone Indians whose chief was Sacagawea's brother. The explorers traded for horses and supplies, and obtained an Indian guide. In what is now Idaho, the Nez Percé welcomed the explorers and even prepared a feast of buffalo and salmon for them. In return, the explorers gave them valuable gifts, such as tobacco and cloth.

Lewis and Clark returned to St. Louis in September of 1806 to welcoming cheers of the city's residents. They brought with them maps of their routes and the surrounding regions, descriptions of plants and animals, as well as information about native peoples of the West.

To Do

Challenge students to create a travel brochure to convince people to move west, following the path of Lewis and Clark. Distribute construction paper to each student. Have students fold the paper into three parts so that it looks like a brochure. On the cover, have students draw a picture of something one might see while traveling west and add a catchy slogan for the title.

In one section of the brochure, have students include a map of Lewis and Clark's route, marking important dates and land features on the map. (Visit www.lewisclark.net/maps/index.html or www.lewis-clark.org/map_main.htm for reference.)

For the other two sections, have students write the following headings, making sure they fill in the rest of the information:

• Looking for adventure? Here's a great reason to travel West:

• Along the way, you'll see these beautiful sights:

On the back cover, have students draw another picture of something one might see out West. Then tell people why they should travel to see the real thing.

Display students' finished brochures on a bulletin board.

The Ballad of Bronco Charlie
(Westward Expansion)

Bronco Charlie was one of 70 adventurous young men who mounted ponies and set off on the Pony Express. For nearly two years, beginning on April 3, 1860, they carried the U.S. mail back and forth along a 1,996-mile relay route that stretched from St. Joseph, Missouri, to Sacramento, California. Riding day and night through rain, snow, and blistering heat, Pony Express riders overcame dangerous obstacles. They crossed hostile Native American territory, treacherous mountains, and barren deserts to deliver the mail in ten days, sometimes less. Other mail routes by sea or land took weeks, even months.

The need for a fast and dependable mail service in the West had become imperative. In 1848, the United States gained what are now Texas, New Mexico, Arizona, California, Nevada, Utah, and most of Colorado when it defeated Mexico in the Mexican-American War. That same year, hundreds of thousands of settlers seeking a better life headed west after the California Gold Rush of 1848. New York City journalist John L. O'Sullivan wrote in 1845 that it is "our manifest destiny to overspread the continent allotted by Providence for the free development of our yearly multiplying millions."

But arguments over whether the new territories should be slave or free states led the young republic closer to civil war. By 1860, half a million people lived in California, and they were hungry for news from the East, especially when talk of war between the North and South escalated. The Pony Express was so important it became a frontier legend. But only two years after it started, new technology replaced it. The ponies made their last run October 26, 1861, two days after eastern and western states were connected by a new invention called the telegraph.

To Do

Students can learn a lot about the Pony Express by studying the geography of the route it covered. Photocopy and distribute "Traveling the Pony Express" (page 17) to each student. Have students study the map to answer the questions on the page.

Answers:
   1. Missouri River **2.** Platte and North Platte Rivers **3.** Rocky Mountains
   4. Great Salt Lake and Utah Lake **5.** Great Salt Lake Desert **6.** Sierra Nevada
Mountains **7.** About 2,000 miles

Gettysburg
(Civil War)

From July 1 through July 3, 1863, more than 75,000 Confederate soldiers and 90,000 Union soldiers met in a deadly clash at Gettysburg, Pennsylvania. The battle changed the course of the Civil War and gave the Union army an advantage it held until the end of the war.

The fighting began when the troops met accidentally in the town of Gettysburg. That day, the Confederate army took the town. But the Union army settled into a strong defensive along Culp's Hill, Cemetery Hill, Little Round Top, and Round Top.

On July 2, Confederate General Robert E. Lee tried to roll up Cemetery Hill and break the Union army. He ordered General George Pickett to send about 13,000 men marching in a perfect line formation up the hill in what would become known as Pickett's Charge.

But only a few soldiers reached the top. Most were quickly shot or captured. Barely half the Confederate soldiers who fought in the battle returned to Lee. Those who did barely managed to escape in retreat back to Virginia. The Union army made little effort to follow.

About 4,000 Southerners and more than 3,000 Northerners died in the battle, but tens of thousands more were wounded, missing, or captured. The Confederate army was never able to launch a major offensive again.

To Do

Use the reproducible map on "A Nation Divided" (page 18) to show how the United States was physically divided during the Civil War by slavery. After you pass out the map, ask students to note the differences between this map and a current map of the United States. Then ask students to follow the instructions on the sheet.

Freedom Train
(Underground Railroad)

The Underground Railroad was an informal system that helped slaves escape from slavery to the northern states and Canada in the mid-1800s. But it wasn't underground or a railroad at all. It was a secret system of houses where slaves could find safety on their dangerous journey to freedom.

Places where slaves could find safety were called *stations*. Slaves who traveled from station to station were called *passengers*. The people who led the slaves to freedom were called *conductors*.

The most heavily traveled routes ran through Ohio, Indiana, and western Pennsylvania. Many reached Canada by way of Detroit or Niagara Falls, New York. Others sailed across Lake Erie to Ontario from ports such as Erie, Pennsylvania, and Sandusky, Ohio.

Many people became famous for their work on the Underground Railroad. Thomas Garrett, a Quaker merchant who lived in Wilmington, Delaware, helped more than 2,000 slaves escape. When a court fined Garrett so heavily that he lost all his property, Garrett stood firm in his beliefs. He told the court, "I say to thee and to all in this court room, that if anyone knows a fugitive who wants shelter…send him to Thomas Garrett, and he will befriend him."

The most famous black leader of the Underground Railroad was Harriet Tubman, herself an escaped slave. She returned to the south 19 times and helped about 300 slaves escape to freedom.

But the Underground Railroad also angered many in the South, and contributed to the growing hostility between the North and South that eventually led to the Civil War.

To Do

Many brave people risked their lives in the fight against slavery. Many lost their lives standing up for what they believed was right. Encourage students to research the life of famous abolitionists, such as Harriet Tubman, Frederick Douglass, Sojourner Truth, William Lloyd Garrison, and Harriet Beecher Stowe. Distribute white construction paper to each student. Ask students to draw or paste a picture of their hero on the top half of the paper, then write a paragraph below it, summarizing his or her accomplishments. Display students' finished work on a bulletin board or create a wall of heroes.

Marvelous Machines
(Age of Invention)

Improved production methods, abundant natural resources, and a growing population all helped industry in the United States to increase almost tenfold between 1870 and 1916. By the turn of the century, industrialization transformed commerce, business organization, the environment, the workplace, the home, and everyday life.

With that industrial growth came many new inventions, which led to a variety of new products. The typewriter appeared in 1867, the telephone in 1876, the phonograph in 1877, the electric light in 1879, and the gasoline automobile in 1885.

But it was the automobile that had the greatest impact on the nation's economy. In the early 1900s, Henry Ford began mass-producing cars on assembly lines. Prices for cars dropped and sales soared. The number of automobiles Americans owned jumped from 8,000 in 1900 to almost 3,500,000 in 1916.

Business leaders also learned how to operate and coordinate many different economic activities across broad geographic areas. Businesses became larger and the modern corporation became an important form of business organization.

To Do

Pair up students and ask each pair to choose a famous inventor and research his or her life. Then have one student pretend to be the inventor, and the other a reporter who will interview the inventor just moments after he or she has made his or her biggest discovery. Invite each pair of students to act out the interviews in front of the class.

Where Are We Going?
(Immigration)

The Statue of Liberty in New York Harbor has welcomed millions of immigrants to America. They came to seek their fortunes or to escape war, famine, and persecution. Some were brought here as slaves.

Until the 1880s most immigrants came from northern and western Europe. The Irish arrived in the 1850s, driven from their homes by famine. They took low-paying jobs in factories and as servants. Others came from Germany, Britain, Holland, and Scandinavia. Most of the new immigrants were Catholic, and by 1850, Catholics made up the largest single religious denomination in the United States.

From the mid-1880s until World War I, immigrants from southern, eastern, and central Europe arrived by the millions. Between 1880 and 1914, 22 million people came to the United States, all seeking a better life. They were mostly Poles, Czechs, Russians, Ukrainians, Croatians, and Jews from the Austro-Hungarian and Russian empires. Greeks, Romanians, and Italians arrived in record numbers, too. Poles and Eastern Europeans found work in factories in cities such as Milwaukee and Chicago. By 1910, more than half the population of 18 cities was made up of immigrants. But immigrants didn't all flock to the cities. Many Scandinavians settled farms in the Midwest.

Their huge numbers also evoked anti-immigrant sentiments. In the 1890s Congress tightened immigration laws, and groups such as the American Protective Association urged immigration restriction. In 1924, Congress passed the National Origins Act, which limited the number of newcomers from each country. The law discriminated against southern and eastern Europeans in particular and excluded Asians entirely. Today the largest groups of immigrants are Asians and Hispanics.

To Do

America is a nation of immigrants. One way to illustrate that is to invite students to research their own family history and share it with the class. Distribute large (18-by-24-inch) construction paper to each student. Have students ask their parents and grandparents for help creating a family tree that goes as far back as they can remember. Then encourage students to write an essay about their family history and present it to the class. Display the family trees on a wall.

Name: _____ Date: _____

Explorer Fact Cube

Directions:

1. Cut out the cube template along the dashed lines.

2. Fill out each panel as directed.

3. Fold along the solid lines to form a cube.

4. Glue each tab behind the panel it meets.

GLUE

Explorer Fact Cube

by

_____

(name)

GLUE

GLUE

GLUE

Write a fact about your explorer.

Draw a picture of your explorer here:

Explorer's name: _____

Write a fact about your explorer.

GLUE

GLUE

GLUE

Write a fact about your explorer.

Write a fact about your explorer.

American Revolution Flip Chart

Directions: Cut along the dashed lines so that each question flips back. Make sure not to cut all the way to the left edge of the paper. Glue the left edge of this page on top of a blank sheet of copy paper, making sure both pages are aligned. Flip back each question and write the correct answer underneath.

----

1. Who was the commander in chief of the American army?

----

2. What act passed by the British Parliament required all legal documents, licenses, commercial contracts, newspapers, pamphlets, dice, and playing cards to have a tax stamp?

----

3. What colonial city was the center of the American Revolution?

----

4. Who was the King of England during the Revolutionary War?

----

5. What is the name of the African-American man who died in the Boston Massacre?

----

6. How many chests of tea were dumped into Boston Harbor?

----

7. Which colonial revolutionary led the colonists who disguised themselves as Mohawk Indians during the Boston Tea Party?

Name: _____   Date: _____

Traveling the Pony Express

You can learn a lot about the Pony Express by studying the geography of the route it covered. Where was the Pony Express route most dangerous? How far could riders go in a day? Study the map, then answer the questions below.

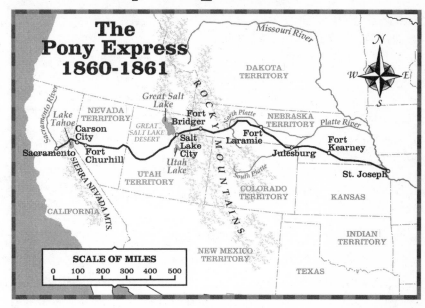

QUESTIONS:

1. The Pony Express began in St. Joseph, Missouri. On what river is St. Joseph located ?

_____

2. Which two rivers did the Pony Express route follow through much of the Nebraska Territory?

_____

3. What major land feature did Pony Express riders cross between the Fort Laramie and Fort Bridger relay stations?

_____

4. Between what two lakes did the Pony Express riders ride in the Utah Territory?

_____

5. What land feature did riders cross just west of these lakes?

_____

6. What mountain range did riders cross in California before finally reaching Sacramento?

_____

7. Approximately how many miles long was the Pony Express?

_____

A Nation Divided

DIRECTIONS:

1. Color the Union states and territories blue: California, Connecticut, Illinois, Indiana, Iowa, Kansas, Maine, Massachusetts, Michigan, Minnesota, New Hampshire, New Jersey, New York, Pennsylvania, Ohio, Oregon, Rhode Island, Wisconsin, Vermont, Colorado Territory, Dakota Territory, Nebraska Territory, Nevada Territory, Utah Territory, and Washington Territory.

2. Color the Confederate states and territories gray: Alabama, Arkansas, Florida, Georgia, Louisiana, Mississippi, North Carolina, South Carolina, Texas, Tennessee, Virginia, New Mexico Territory, Indian Territory (Unorganized Territory).

3. Some slave states remained in the Union. Color those states red: Delaware, Kentucky, Maryland, Missouri, West Virginia.

4. Was the state you live in part of the Union or the Confederacy?

_____

Welcome to the New World

(Exploration)

We came across the ocean in search of fame and fortune,
and landed in the Indies, so we thought.
But much to our astonishment, we found a whole new continent
even better than the one we lost.

CHORUS:
    Welcome to the New World!
    It seems everybody is here.
    There's plenty of room, but you'd better come soon—
    the New World is growing each year,
    and it seems everybody is here.

The French are in Canada, Spain controls Florida,
and they've got most of the West.
King George governs most of the Eastern seacoast,
and he's trying to take all the rest.

CHORUS

The rivers and forests are full of explorers,
all wandering around getting lost.
There's Cortés and Cartier, Hudson and Jolliet,
and they all think they're the boss.

CHORUS

There's gold in the mountains,
and maybe a fountain of youth,
if you know where to look.
There are claims to be staking and fortunes
for making or taking, by hook or by crook.

CHORUS

There are trappers and traders here,
pilgrims and pioneers,
prisoners, pirates, and farmers.
There are doctors and lawyers
and cobblers and sawyers,
what we could use is a barber!

CHORUS

The People of the Land

(Native Americans)

We lived in the forests and in the mountains,
in deerskin tipis and wooden houses.
We were nomads and village dwellers,
living in igloos and earthen shelters.

And we marked the passing of seasons
from the time that time began.
For generations we were the people of the land.
We were the people of the land.

We lived on maize, squash, and beans.
We gathered berries and fished in the streams.
We hunted caribou, elk, and deer,
and looked to the land to provide for our needs.

We played games and we told stories.
We loved to sing and we loved to dance.
From many nations, we were the people of the land.
We were the people of the land.

We were the Choctaw, we were the Cherokee,
We were the Seneca and the Shoshone,
We were the Nez Percé, we were the Navajo,
We were the Apache and the Arapaho.

And we flew like the eagle,
like the buffalo, we ran.
From sea to sea, we were the people of the land.
We were the people of the land.

We are the people of the land.

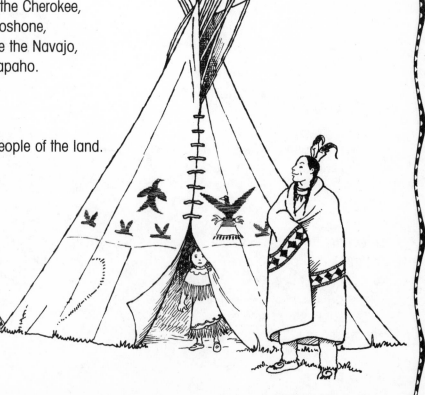

The Tea and the Taxes

(American Revolution)

Listen my children, and you'll hear what happened—
the strangest tea party that you can imagine.
The teapot we used was the harbor of Boston,
and King George sent over the tea.

You see, he wanted us to pick up the expenses—
of paying his army, maintaining defenses—
and the argument came to a head in December of 1773.

CHORUS:
    Now it's hi, ho, over it goes, into the Boston Harbor.
    With hatchets and axes, the tea and the taxes
    went into the Boston Harbor.

We couldn't vote, but they made us pay taxes
on sugar and paper, on glass and molasses,
the lead in our bullets, the paint on our houses.
We even paid taxes on stamps.

turn the page

The Tea and the Taxes

(continued)

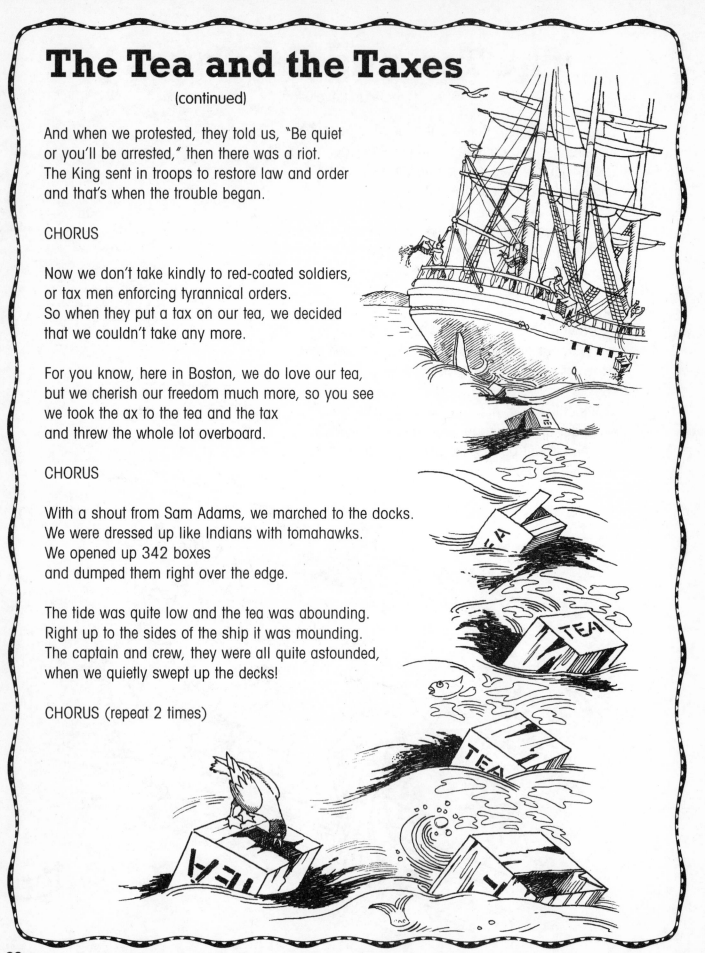

And when we protested, they told us, "Be quiet
or you'll be arrested," then there was a riot.
The King sent in troops to restore law and order
and that's when the trouble began.

CHORUS

Now we don't take kindly to red-coated soldiers,
or tax men enforcing tyrannical orders.
So when they put a tax on our tea, we decided
that we couldn't take any more.

For you know, here in Boston, we do love our tea,
but we cherish our freedom much more, so you see
we took the ax to the tea and the tax
and threw the whole lot overboard.

CHORUS

With a shout from Sam Adams, we marched to the docks.
We were dressed up like Indians with tomahawks.
We opened up 342 boxes
and dumped them right over the edge.

The tide was quite low and the tea was abounding.
Right up to the sides of the ship it was mounding.
The captain and crew, they were all quite astounded,
when we quietly swept up the decks!

CHORUS (repeat 2 times)

The Bill of Rights Rag

(Bill of Rights)

Freedom of religion, freedom of speech,
freedom of the press, and the right to meet
together, to talk about our gripes—
it's in the Bill of Rights.

The first ten amendments to the Constitution
are the rights that we won in the revolution.
The founding fathers wrote them down in black and white.
It's all right there in the Bill of Rights.

They can't put soldiers up in your house.
They can't come knocking and shake you down
without permission, in the day or night.
It's in the Bill of Rights.

turn the page

The Bill of Rights Rag

(continued)

The Fifth Amendment says you can't be pressured
to testify against yourself if you're arrested.
Everybody gets a fair and speedy trial.
It says so there in the Bill of Rights.

The Bill of Rights…they're there when you need 'em.
The Bill of Rights…the Constitution guaranteed 'em.
The Bill of Rights…it's all about freedom.
Let's hear three cheers for the Bill of Rights!

The Eighth Amendment says always try
to make sure the punishment fits the crime
and don't set bail or fines too high.
It's in the Bill of Rights.

And any other rights we forgot to mention
belong to the people or the ones they elected
to represent them to the powers on high.
That's what it says in the Bill of Rights.

Grand Adventure

(Lewis & Clark)

Lewis and Clark on a mission exploratory
boldly searched the great unknown.
They crossed the vast Louisiana Territory,
looking for a route to the western shore.

President Jefferson sent them on the trip.
He told them, "Keep your eyes open, tell me what you find."
Maybe there'll be unicorns, seven-foot beavers,
maybe prehistoric creatures, legendary lost tribes.

CHORUS:
    What a grand adventure, what a traveler's dream,
    seeing sights hardly anyone had ever seen.
    From the mighty Mississippi to the western sea,
    it was a grand adventure indeed.

They left St. Louis in the spring of 'aught-four
up the wild Missouri in a wooden riverboat,
thirty-three men, two horses, and a dog,
a compass, and twelve pounds of soap.

They spent the winter with the Mandan people
in the land of the Dakotas, where they took a little rest.
They met a young woman named Sacagawea
and she went along with them when they headed on west.

They took a wrong turn in mid-Montana.
But with Sacagawea acting as their guide,
they came to the foot of the Rocky Mountains
and made their way across the Continental Divide.

turn the page

Grand Adventure

(continued)

The trail was treacherous, long and hard,
and they nearly starved, nearly froze to death.
But then in the distance, they saw the Pacific
and they knew that they had made it all the way to the West.

It was a long, wet winter, on the western shore,
three thousand miles away from home.
It rained for weeks, then it rained some more,
and in the spring they couldn't wait to go home.

They crossed the mountains and hurried back east
They couldn't wait to tell of all the things they'd seen:
prairie dogs, antelope, vast herds of buffalo,
and great big grizzly bears the size of trees.

The people all cheered when they saw them coming,
'cause everybody figured that they must have died.
After twenty-eight months, they returned home heroes,
having traveled pretty nearly 8,000 miles.

CHORUS (repeat 2 times)

The Ballad of Bronco Charlie

(Westward Expansion)

My name is Bronco Charlie, I rode the Pony Express.
We started in Missouri and took those ponies west,
for twenty-five dollars weekly and a chance to ride the wind.
If I were young I'd do it all again.

We rode through rain and thunder, across the prairie wide,
with arrows flying 'round us, trouble on every side.
We risked our necks delivering news and carrying the mail,
no matter what, we did it without fail.

CHORUS: It was twenty-five miles between the stations—
        the fastest means of communication
        from the East Coast clear out to the West.
        What a great old, glorious story— the Pony Express.

I started at eleven, weighed barely 90 pounds,
but I was proud to ride with the bravest men around.
Like good old Wild Bill Hickok and the famous Buffalo Bill,
We galloped over deserts, sand, and hills.

Through the Western Territories, on the path of pioneers,
all the way to Sacramento, where we were met with cheers.
Two thousand miles of rugged riding in the rain or shine,
Summer, winter, in the day or night.

CHORUS

We carried all the latest news to the western shore—
Abe Lincoln's first election and the start of Civil War—
in half the time it used to take for news to reach the West.
We made the trip in ten days, maybe less.

But when they strung the telegraph, it made us obsolete
With letters flying over wires, how could we compete?
That was the final chapter of the bravest and the best,
who rode into the history of the West.

CHORUS

Gettysburg

(Civil War)

We came from Massachusetts, we came from Tennessee,
and we met in Pennsylvania, in July of '63.
In a place called Gettysburg, just a quiet little country town,
the armies of the North and South, and we laid our bodies down.

CHORUS:
  O little town of Gettysburg,
  how still we see thee lie,
  now that the battle is over,
  and the storm has passed us by.

The thunder of the cannons shook the earth beneath our feet.
The smoke from all the shooting was so thick, we couldn't see.
And marching through those open fields, men and boys in blue and gray,
like stalks of wheat in endless rows, fell before the reaper's blade.

CHORUS

We were fighting for the Union.
We were fighting for our rights.
But in that little Pennsylvania town,
we were mostly fighting for our lives.

Some of them were strangers,
some of them were friends.
Sometimes you couldn't tell the difference,
you could only pray that it would end soon.

By the time that it was over, on the fourth of July,
fifty thousand men had fallen, as the rain fell from the sky.
They say it was the turning point of that bloody Civil War,
but at the time, it was hard to remember what we were even fighting for.

CHORUS

Freedom Train

(Underground Railroad)

I'm riding on a train, and I don't know where I'm bound.
I don't know the conductor's name, or when I'll reach the next town.
I can't see the road ahead, haven't seen a friendly face,
but I can see a bright star shining, leading me to a better place.

CHORUS
   And the name of the train is freedom.
   It's the train out of slavery.
   I'm on the train to freedom,
   and soon I will be free.

This train doesn't have an engine, doesn't have an engineer.
It doesn't ride on iron rails, there's no coal or freight cars here.
It never runs through town, and it only runs at night.
Got to keep this railroad secret, keep the passengers out of sight.

CHORUS

Everything I own is right here in this sack,
and when I reach the border, I won't be coming back.
I can hear the hunter's shout, and the barking of the hounds.
I'm hungry, cold, and weary, but this train ain't stopping now.

CHORUS (repeat 2 times)

Marvelous Machines

(The Age of Invention)

A new day is dawning and everything's changing
as brand new inventions keep coming our way.
The folks in the past never could have imagined
the wonders we see every day.

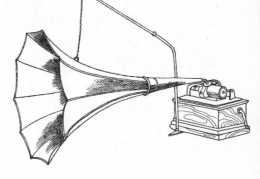

We can watch moving pictures right there on the screen,
hear music play on a talking machine.
Our houses are spotless, our clothes are all clean,
and it's thanks to those marvelous machines!

The typewriter makes letter writing so easy.
Disposable razors give a good, clean shave.
The mimeograph makes printing so speedy,
think of all the time that we save!

We can soar like a bird in a flying machine,
talk to Aunt Clara, out in Abilene.
We've got news on the hour by radio beam,
and it's thanks to those marvelous machines!

turn the page

Marvelous Machines

(continued)

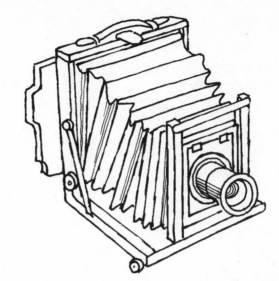

The wonders of communication,
travel, and illumination,
all are cause for celebration.
And we're not through yet!

Miracles of transportation,
industry, and aviation,
give us time to take vacations.
What will they do next?

Now we can take pictures by pressing a button,
and turn on a light at the flick of a switch.
The electric icebox, the iron, and oven,
are changing the way that we live.

It's the age of invention, the era of dreams,
full of gadgets and gizmos like you've never seen,
fantastic ideas and ridiculous schemes,
and it's thanks to those marvelous, fabulous,
glorious, wonderful, marvelous machines!

Where Are We Going?

(Immigration)

Where are we going?
What will we see?
And when we get there
who will we be?

We left our homeland
and crossed the sea.
We were so tired
but we still had dreams.

We dreamed of work.
We dreamed of food.
We dreamed of freedom
to live as we choose.

And then we saw her
holding the flame—
twelve million people,
and still we came.

Where are we going?
What will we see?
And when we get there
who will we be?